3% LEADER

—

THE PROVEN SYSTEM *for*
TOP TIER PERFORMANCE

WRITTEN BY CAREY L. ROME, EXECUTIVE MANAGEMENT CONSULTANT
AND CREATOR OF THE 3% LEADER™ SYSTEM.

INTRODUCTION

Some schools of thought maintain that leadership is something with which we're born. In other words, some of us possess an innate ability to successfully and effectively lead others. Perhaps that's true to some degree, but for the majority of us, leadership is a skill that takes time, work and discipline to develop.

Over the past 15 years that I've been working with organizational leaders, I've found the most successful ones have some common traits. Successful leaders continually strive for improvement, work hard at keeping their skills sharp and always look for better, more effective ways to motivate and lead teams and/or organizations.

Those are no doubt laudable traits; however, from my perspective, these are leadership ABCs. They comprise only a part of the necessary package to become a transformational leader – one who can lead his or her organization out of turbulence and uncertainty, and into consistent, sustained success and excellence.

Top tier performers complement their God-given "abilities" with a secret – a systematic, deliberate process to achieve their success. This blend of leadership traits and disciplined process forms the foundation of our assertion that Leadership is a system. Through our 3% Leader System™, we've demystified and simplified the secrets of top tier leaders for you to use as your springboard.

So, why 3%?

Early in my career and work with leaders, I came across a somewhat infamous study conducted on the 1979 Harvard MBA program, most recently noted in the April 2014 Forbes article, "Why You Should Be Writing Down Your Goals." [8]

In the study[9], students were asked three questions:
1. Do you have or set goals?
2. Are your goals in writing?
3. Are your goals clear, and have you made specific plans to accomplish them?

The study's initial findings were:
» 84 percent had no goals at all.
» 13 percent had goals, but they weren't in writing.
» Only 3 percent had written goals and plans to achieve them.

Ten years later, a follow-up to the study cited two key findings:
» The 13 percent of the class who had goals, but did not write them down, earned twice the amount of the 84

---

8 "Why You Should Be Writing Down Your Goals" by Ashley Feinstein, Forbes, April 8, 2014

9 "Why 3% of Harvard MBAs Make Ten Times as Much as the Other 97% Combined" article posted by Sid Savara.
"What They Don't Teach You At Harvard Business School: Notes From A Street-Smart Executive" by Mark McCormack, published in 1984 by Bantam.

percent who had no goals.

» The 3 percent who had written goals with accompanying plans were earning, on average, 10 times as much as the other 97 percent of the class combined.

I was intrigued by that "3 percent," and in fact, as I looked to validate this often-referenced study, I continued to come strikingly close to a 3 percent rule in further readings and in my own work. For example, Stephen Shapiro, author of "Goal-free Living,"[10] in his research conducted with the help of the Opinion Corporation of Princeton, N.J., found that:

» 45 percent of Americans usually set New Year's resolutions.

» Of the 45 percent, only 8 percent of people are always successful in achieving their resolutions.

Said another way, 8 percent of the 45 percent set goals and achieve them. The math works out to 3.6 percent (.08*.45).

Let's look at it from a simple sports analogy – 2.9 percent of high school athletes continue on to play collegiate basketball.[11]

And lastly, you've probably heard that third-generation business owners tend to squander the success built by

---

10 "Goal-Free Living: How to Have the Life You Want NOW!" by Stephen M. Shapiro, published 2006 by John Wiley & Sons, Inc.

11 Teacherweb.com (White Station High School)

their predecessors. Well, not entirely. You guessed it: A mere 3 percent of third generation companies continues to remain profitable.[12]

There are many other instances where the 3 percent rule has held true, so much so that I began to explore it as a basis for leadership methodology, and ultimately developed the concepts and principles around the 3% Leader System.

At its foundation, the 3% Leader approach is designed to help you as a leader establish a deliberate approach for executing a successful strategy and achieving your vision and goals. It demystifies top-performing executives' methods to success, and helps you create your own.

To understand how a leader might become more deliberate in establishing his or her approach, it may be helpful to understand our very specific definition of a 3% Leader. The 3% Leader is one who deliberately and intentionally designs and focuses daily on the tasks required to successfully achieve overall goals, implement strategy and materialize his or her vision.

Simple as this may sound, most executives struggle to articulate their vision, establish an executable strategy and build a roadmap detailing how success will be achieved. Consequently, tactical and targeted execution becomes virtually impossible.

---

[12] "Why Most Families Lose Their Wealth by the Third Generation," by Tim Voorhees, JD, MBA, WealthCounsel

Without a simple system to follow, many leaders waste time, and eventually plateau. Over time, they become less and less valuable to the organization. This makes you vulnerable to downsizing and reorganizations.

When I was beginning my career, one of my biggest fears in life was to be 50 years old, (a very vulnerable time in a professional's life) and get fired. This happens every day – just when your kids are in college, just when you are making more money than ever and just when you can see the retirement finish line.

This fear is not unique to me. According to an Urban Institute study published last year[13], workers in their fifties are about 20% less likely than workers ages 25-34 to become re-employed. That's a sobering statistic but look at this graphical representation from the California Department of Human Resources. The drop in employment at age 50 is frightening.[14]

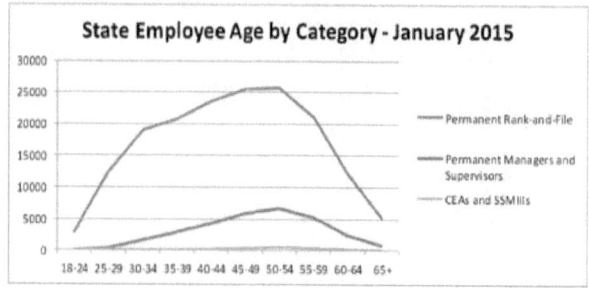

---

13 "Workers over 50 are the new 'unemployables.'" by Annalyn Kurtz, CNN Money, Feb. 26. 2013.

14 California Department of Human Resources: State Demographics and Labor Statistics: January 2015 State Employee Age Demographics

So, how can you keep yourself from getting lulled to sleep? You have to keep yourself in the game.

3% Leaders possess a unique perspective – they view their tasks and activities through the lens of the vision they want to achieve for their organization, not through the lens of the latest or biggest fire. This perspective is a critical difference.

One very relatable way about which to think of 3% Leadership is in the realm of professional athletes. The most successful professional athletes have a vision for what they want to achieve. They implement a strategy to achieve that vision. They establish goals so that they can mark milestones along the journey, and they isolate exactly what they need to deliberately practice. Successful professional athletes get the resources they need, and they measure their success.

> Leaders possess a unique perspective -- they view their daily tasks and activities through the lens of their vision for their organization, not through the lens of the latest or biggest fire.

Let's use Peyton Manning as an example. If Peyton's vision is to win a Super Bowl, he has probably determined that given his abilities, he's best picking defenses apart eight yards at a time. So Peyton builds a strategy around picking defenses apart eight yards at a time. He builds an offense to achieve this type of strategy and sets tactical steps to meticulously study film. The process of reviewing film enables Peyton to view his team through the lens of his eight-yard strategy and his vision. This creates focus.

Not all that different than in the business world, is it?

The 3% Leader concept illustrated by professional athletes has been proven time and time again. The question is: Why don't business leaders train more like professional athletes?

I believe the answer lies in the complexity of achieving both individual and business goals. This e-book works to break down that complexity and lays out a holistic methodology and system designed to help you refine your own distinct approach to management excellence.

Leaders who implement and follow the 11 principles of the 3% Leader System enjoy clarity of direction, team alignment and, ultimately, are able to do more. Success builds on success which will build unstoppable momentum.

TABLE OF CONTENTS

Module 1 - Think
    Principle 1. Lead From Within
    Principle 2. Establish Your Core
    Principle 3. Stake Your Non-negotiables
    Principle 4. Build Your Boundaries
    Principle 5. Address Your Fears

Module 2 - Solve
    Principle 6. Crystallize Your Vision
    Principle 7. Map Your Strategy
    Principle 8. Align Your Goals

Module 3 - Start
    Principle 9. Implement Digestible Projects
    Principle 10. Align Your Resources
    Principle 11. Measure What Matters

Conclusion:
    Implementing Leadership as a System

PRINCIPLE 1. LEAD FROM WITHIN

The most effective leaders know themselves – their strengths, limitations and how to leverage what they have for individual and organizational success.

Jerry Rice, possibly one of the all-time best players in the National Football League (NFL), knew exactly who he was. Rice understood his strengths, and just as important, knew his limitations. For this reason, Rice designed every practice to work on specific areas to compensate for, or overcome them.

"Rice didn't need to do everything well, just certain things. He had to run precise patterns; he had to evade the defenders, sometimes two or three, who were assigned to cover him; he had to out-jump them to catch the ball and outmuscle them when they tried to strip it away; then he had to outrun tacklers. So he focused his practice work on exactly these requirements." – Geoff Colvin, **Talent is Overrated**.[8]

Professional athletes who achieve the pinnacle of their careers, focus on knowing themselves through and through. These athletes build a deliberate plan to accomplish their goals, taking into account their limitations. In our world, as well as the pro athlete's world, limitations are not an excuse. Known limitations actually help us build a plan for success.

---

[8] "Talent Is Overrated: What Really Separates World-Class Performers from Everybody Else" by Geoff Colvin, published 2008 by Portfolio (Penguin Group)

In my experience, however, business leaders struggle with this more than anything. We tend to practice what we do well. But without understanding our limitations, our default mode is to overemphasize what we do know. Consequently, we continue doing things the way we've always done them. Unfortunately, this habit generates a plateau by lulling you into complacency. If the focus is status quo, what are you leaving left undone? How does this gap create limitations to your value?

"*You don't get benefits from mechanical repetition, but by adjusting your execution over and over to get closer to your goal. You have to tweak the system by pushing, allowing for more errors at first as you increase your limits.*" – Anders Ericsson, the psychologist behind the **10,000 Hour Rule**.[9]

Once you fully understand your strengths and limitations, you're in a better position to communicate your expectations to your teams. Determining **what you want from your team**, in the context of **who you are**, is foundational to 3% Leadership.

> Determining what you want from your team, in the context of who you are, is foundational to 3% Leadership.

There are many tests that exist to help you identify your strengths and weaknesses. We utilize principles 2 – 5 to

---

9 "Masters of Habit: The Deliberate Practice and Training of Jerry Rice" article by James Clear

help you think through your leadership style. However, as a starting point, it's helpful to pinpoint your natural personality tendencies. Whether you use Gallup Strengths Center, Myers Briggs, DISC or some other assessment tool, establishing a baseline is a critical building block for Principles 2 – 11.

PRINCIPLE 2. ESTABLISH YOUR CORE

Solidifying what you stand for is integral to your success as a leader.

Having identified your strengths and limitations, it's logical to next consider what motivates or inspires you. Are you drawn to leaders who accomplish their goals at all costs regardless of the damage or destruction left behind? Or are you more impressed by leaders who accomplish their goals with an army of team members who would run through a brick wall for them? Using our professional athlete analogy, scores of professional athletes lie and cheat every year in order to be seen as successful. But when the dust settles, who do we remember most? Typically, we remember the leaders and athletes who achieve their success with character.

For a real-life example of this, I encourage you to view the acceptance speech of Kevin Durant when he received the 2013-2014 NBA Most Valuable Player award. After watching this clip, there is no question in my mind that Kevin Durant is a 3% Leader and a man of character.

Conversely, we have all worked for those leaders who are perceived as purely self-serving – always taking credit, never at fault and consistently fostering politics. Other leaders are seen as viewing their employees as stepping stones on the path to success. I call these "me-oriented" leaders. And as we all know, in the long run, people get tired of a "me-oriented" leader.

There are also leaders who attempt to be "everything to

everyone." This style of leadership leaves a team confused about what the leader actually stands for. Obviously, "people pleasers" are the serial offenders here, but this trait is not unique to them. Many well-intentioned leaders fall into this trap because they simply underestimate the importance of their teams knowing what they stand for – understanding their core.

How do you identify your core? Here's one exercise I recommend: Ask yourself the following: What are the three things that you want everyone to say about you when you are not around? For example, would they reference you as a "good guy?" (a phrase that has been so over-used that it is now meaningless) Or will they state specifics? (i.e., Jim is a fair but firm leader. His strength is developing people.) The three desired attributes answering your question comprise your "core," and will become your guidepost as a leader. Your core is what keeps you grounded through both wild success and tragic defeat.

The trick for leaders is to be real. Force yourself to narrow down three leadership characteristics that you intend to embody. No more than three. Now, live and breathe these characteristics in every action you take with your employees, and you will be amazed at the trust you begin to build.

You may also consider this from another angle: Have you ever met someone you didn't necessarily like but respected nonetheless? Why is that? More than likely, you disagree with his or her stance, but at least you know where the person stands. Now, contrast that with a leader who is unclear of his or her convictions. With whom would you rather work?

I can't emphasize enough that the traits that make up your core should never be compromised. Camouflaged in the pretty wrappings of "opportunity" are things that will cause you to be tempted to compromise your core. While easily justified, small compromises to your core are virtually impossible to overcome. In some cases, you may lose the trust of a team member who eventually becomes a vocal detractor. We all know office politics are a nasty reality.

Establishing your core means focusing on what you believe is most important and ignoring the detractors. Everyone may not like it, but if you stay true to your core, everyone will respect what you stand for.

> Camouflaged in the pretty wrappings of "opportunity" are things that will cause you to be tempted to compromise your core. While easily justified, small compromises to your core are virtually impossible to overcome.

PRINCIPLE 3. STAKE YOUR NON-NEGOTIABLES

Non-negotiables are the standards of acceptable behavior by which 3% Leaders live.

How many professional athletes and executives have we seen achieve greatness only to be crumpled by their lack of morals or character? The list is long. I believe professional athletes and executives at the top of their game who destroy themselves and their image do so because they fail to set and live by non-negotiables.

Setting non-negotiables is not a new concept, but it is one that has been watered down tremendously. Whether you call them values, guidelines or principles, 3% Leaders firmly establish a line in the sand and never cross it. Your non-negotiables do not have to be unique. However, what should remain unique is your willingness to hold true to your word.

> Your non-negotiables do not have to be unique. However, what should remain unique is your willingness to hold true to your word.

Here's a good analogy to help you think of the importance of non-negotiables. Think of a utility pole that must be firmly planted in solid ground for power to be distributed. If you're looking up at the utility pole, think of the amount of power running to the left and right off the top of the pole and the amount of revenue being generated. Now, what happens if that one utility pole comes down? Power is disrupted and the ripple effect is tremendous.

So it is when a leader "breaks" a non-negotiable. That lapse minimizes or halts the leader's effectiveness. Essentially, a lack of established non-negotiables prevents a leader from having influence. While a leader's power to influence begins with core, it is solidified with non-negotiables.

PRINCIPLE 4. BUILD YOUR BOUNDARIES

3% Leaders set and respect the boundaries that enable them and their teams to operate most successfully.

How many times have we witnessed the best athlete on the field attempt to do everything, yet, his or her team still fails? Conversely, let's consider athletes such as pro football players Tom Brady and Peyton Manning. Neither would ever be considered the most athletic player on the field (typically defined as the fastest, most nimble and versatile). However, both are considered exceptional leaders and all-time greats in the NFL. Why is that?

Both Brady and Manning have specific boundaries as players, and their teammates know their boundaries. Brady and Manning are pocket quarterbacks. They rely on their offensive lines for protection, and they rarely scramble. Brady and Manning have established consistent boundaries for what they do and don't do. This allows other teammates to understand their own roles more clearly and perform better.

3% Leaders are like Brady and Manning. They create consistent boundaries within which they operate, allowing other teammates to better understand where they fit in and consequently perform at higher levels.

Translate that to your own situation. Realistically, leaders can't make or be involved in every decision and still create a scalable organization. So as a leader, you have a choice: Make every decision yourself and limit your growth, or entrust others to make decisions within certain parameters.

> Creating boundaries means leading your team with trust.

Creating boundaries means leading your team with trust. When leaders extend trust first, they build tremendous confidence in their teams and vice versa. Allow team members to make some decisions – and some mistakes – within the boundaries you have established and communicated clearly.

PRINCIPLE 5. ADDRESS YOUR FEARS

3% Leaders understand how to balance risks and fears by leveraging resources to obtain their goals.

I am certain pro baseball player Maury Wills had a deep fear that he would never make it to the majors. But Maury changed the game by taking a huge risk that ultimately made him one of Major League Baseball's most memorable base runners. There is no doubt that Wills had a vision of playing in the majors. However, after 10 years in the minors, he continued to struggle because of his batting. In order for Wills to effectively use his greatest gift, speed, he needed to get on base. Understanding specifically what he needed to focus on, Wills accepted a risk – changing the way he hit. He identified the resources (specific batting expertise) he would need to be successful. Taking the advice of one of his coaches, he learned a new batting technique that allowed him to get on base more often to maximize his speed.

Wills developed a unique method for base-stealing that rattled pitchers, went on to break Ty Cobb's record for stolen bases in one year and helped lead his team to three World Series. All of this was possible because Wills accepted the risk of changing in order to take the next step, leverage resources and achieve his goals.

Leaders often view risk only in the context of business. However, risk is inherent in leadership: An organization's lack of success will ultimately land on the desk of a leader. 3% Leaders understand where the buck stops and accept this risk. For a leader's team to follow him or her on the journey to achieve the vision, the risks of leading must be accepted.

> Without acknowledging and accepting the risks and fears faced as a leader, these risks become excuses never to get started.

Without acknowledging and accepting the risks and fears faced as a leader, these risks become excuses never to get started. Your team will sense hesitancy, excuses will create indecision and your vision will remain a dream.

PRINCIPLE 6. CRYSTALLIZE YOUR VISION

3% Leaders are skilled at providing clarity for and sharing their vision. As a result, they leave a legacy.

Professional athletes have a vision of what they want to accomplish. In describing their vision, these athletes specifically state, "in X number of years I am going to..." That is vision. I find this intriguing because most think vision is only something done at a corporate level.

As leaders, we conceptually know what vision is, and we often hear a lot of rhetoric around it. Unfortunately, many leaders buy into the rhetoric or attempt to copy the vision of others.

3% Leaders take their foundational elements (Core, Non-negotiables, Boundaries, Risks and Resources) and create something unique that they want to achieve with and for their organizations. Consider it another way: The average leader performs good work but not something that couldn't be replaced by the next leader with similar skills. 3% Leaders leave a legacy.

Peter Drucker and Jack Welch sum it up best with these two quotes:

"Management is doing things right; leadership is doing the right things." ~ Peter Drucker[10]

---

10   "Essential Drucker: Management, the Individual, and Society" by Peter Drucker, published 2001 by HarperCollins Publishers

"Good business leaders create a vision, articulate the vision, passionately own the vision, and relentlessly drive it to completion." ~ Jack Welch[11]

Peter Drucker was right: Management is about doing things right. And, never think there is not value in management. There undoubtedly is, just not as much value as in true leadership. If leadership is doing the "right things," what are those right things? For the 3% Leader, the right things are tied to the leader's vision.

Where do you begin? Simply start with saying, "I want to _____" in the next three years.

Those simple words start the process of crystallizing your vision. An exercise on which I have 3% Leaders focus centers around a three year 'I want to?' list. Quite literally, I have executives make a list of what they want to accomplish. Our approach is retrospective: "If you look back in three years, what would you have liked to accomplish with your organization?"

So start your three-year list. Brainstorm. Put your ideas on the whiteboard. Or, if you're like me, take a long walk, and record or capture thoughts as they come to you. Do whatever it takes to free your mind from the constraints of the four walls in your office.

Let's face it, vision is hard. It is not uncommon for leaders

---

11   "Good business leaders create a vision, articulate the vision, passionately own the vision, and relentlessly drive it to completion." ~ Jack Welch

to struggle with the point of creating a vision. In a world where technology can provide us with the answers to any question at the tip of our fingers, vision takes time. Vision takes thinking creatively. Vision takes flexibility in traditional thought processes.

3% Leaders create vision by using the foundational elements they have solidified – Core, Non-negotiables, Boundaries, Risks and Resources – as springboards to cultivate fresh ideas.

With the vision crystallized or clarified, the leader's next primary responsibility is framing up the strategy required to achieve the vision.

3% Leaders rely on their management team assessment of the time, money and resources required for the vision. This high-level exercise and clear communication gives credence to the leader's vision. Target dates, estimated investment and emphasizing the resources you'll require lets your team know that your vision is more than a dream.

PRINCIPLE 7. MAP YOUR STRATEGY

3% Leaders methodically lay out the short- and long-term strategy to execute on their vision.

Creating your vision is only half the job. To truly be successful, you must articulate it and share it with your team. This entails mapping your vision (what you'd like to accomplish) to your strategy (how you're going to accomplish it). Strategy can be most simply defined as the process of turning your vision into a reality. Everyone must chart the path to achieve his or her vision or it will not happen.

To help articulate this to your team, think of a prism. Your job is to communicate your vision and strategy with such clarity that it projects energy and light throughout the organization. Just as a prism projects myriad colors, your vision should create discrete pinpointed lanes, facets of focused effort that your team will undertake to achieve your vision. Each of these facets of focused effort represents how each individual in a group will accomplish your vision. Clarity is critical. If your team members can't clearly understand how the work they need to perform ties to your vision, realignment is needed.

> If your team members can't clearly understand how the work they need to perform ties to your vision, realignment is needed.

Athletes don't often use the word strategy, but that does not mean they don't have one. Kareem Abdul-Jabbar worked to perfect the hook shot. As a tactic to execute his strategy, Peyton Manning systematically studies film of opposing defenses to perfect play-calling at the line. And, to perfect his base stealing, Maury Wills studied pitchers' tendencies. Each of these professionals had a vision.

The strategy of how they achieve this vision is evident in their methodical and deliberate practice of certain things.

Strategy is an over-used word. We live in a very dynamic world with change happening faster than ever before. For this reason, 3% Leaders execute a 12-month strategy while continuously forecasting out an additional 12 months.

While the concept of a "12 plus12" rolling strategy sounds strange to some, it's a relief to many. Strategy taken in the context of three years can seem too inflexible given the rate of change in today's business environment. On the other hand, succumbing to noncommittal trends "because the world just moves too fast" will lead you down a curvy path to nowhere.

Consequently, 3% Leaders think of vision in terms of three years, and strategy in terms of two years (12 plus12). In doing this, 3% Leaders accept the reality that the rate at which information is received is faster than ever. They also recognize that you can be focused on a strategy without giving up the nimble responsiveness required in today's business environment.

PRINCIPLE 8. ALIGN YOUR GOALS

3% Leaders set specific goals that are designed to purposely address those things that are required to execute their strategy and achieve their vision.

"When I got cut from the varsity team as a sophomore in high school, I learned something. I knew I never wanted to feel that bad again. So I set a goal of becoming a starter on the varsity. That's what I focused on all summer. When I worked on my game, that's what I thought about. When it happened, I set another goal, a reasonable, manageable goal that I could realistically achieve if I worked hard enough. I guess I approached it with the end in mind. I knew exactly where I wanted to go, and I focused on getting there. As I reached those goals, they built on one another. I gained a little confidence every time I came through." – Michael Jordan[12]

Let's talk about goals. We've all heard the preaching about goals, and in fact: People who set goals are X times wealthier than those who don't ... Write down your goals... Look at your goals every day ... Tell someone about your goals. And on, and on, and on.

Don't mistake me, goals are foundational to 3% Leaders. There is often a fundamental problem, however, with all the discussion around goals in that they never become real. Most goal-setting exercises prompt more dreaming than determining how to achieve the goal. Average-

---

[12] "I Can't Accept Not Trying: Michael Jordan on the Pursuit of Excellence" by Michael Jordan, published 1994 by HarperCollins Publishers

performing leaders set generic goals, which are measured in very general terms, and they get about average results.

3% Leaders have a process that is contrary to most of what you hear as it relates to goals. How often have you heard to be specific when writing down your goals? The point is well-intentioned, but gets complicated with multiple goals across business, personal and spiritual aspects of life. For this reason, 3% Leaders start with vision and then drill down into goal-setting.

They set specific goals that are designed to purposely address those areas that are required to execute their strategy and achieve their vision. Specific goals get measured with precision on a regular basis. In doing this, 3% Leaders isolate what needs to be improved and they adjust their goals accordingly.

Set your goals in the *context* of your vision, but viewed through a 12-month lens. Do this by determining if the following statement holds true:

> Set your goals in the context of your vision, but viewed through a 12-month lens.

"If in the next 12 months I were to accomplish these X things, I would consider myself on the right path to executing my strategy and achieving my vision."

Your 12-month goals should be building blocks. As such,

it is critical that your goals be set sequentially to prevent future rework. Each day, month and quarter you are building the foundation for your vision.

PRINCIPLE 9. IMPLEMENT DIGESTIBLE PROJECTS

3% Leaders view a project as a specific thing that needs to be accomplished to achieve a particular part of a goal and brings them closer to their vision.

The word "project" is over-used in the corporate world and with leaders. In fact, if there is ever a term that deserves an air quote, it's "project." However, while it might be over-used by the world, 3% Leaders are very intentional in its use.

3% Leaders view a project as a specific thing that needs to be accomplished to achieve a particular part of a goal, ultimately bringing them closer to their vision.

Let's consider the well-known example of Michael Phelps. Phelps had a vision of becoming the most decorated Olympian of all time in swimming. To help Phelps achieve this vision, one of the projects his coach incorporated into practice was having Phelps swim blindfolded. This accomplished two things: 1) helped Phelps focus on his number of strokes for the length of the pool and 2) prepared him for water getting into his goggles. By incorporating this project (i.e., something specific that needed to be accomplished to achieve a particular part of a goal) within his practice, Phelps developed a habit of not relying on sight.

We all know the rest of the story. Michael Phelps made history by winning his fourth gold medal in the Beijing Games — an historical medal of his career — by swimming blind.

"I dove in and (my goggles) filled up with water, and it got worse and worse during the race. From the 150-meter wall to the finish, I couldn't see the wall. I was just hoping I was winning," Phelps said in a post-race interview.[13]

Here's the point: Without the specific project (swimming blindfolded which was designed to help Phelps deal with adversity,) it is likely that Phelps may not have achieved his goal. It is clear that Phelps' coach's strategy was to balance routine in practice with adversity. That strategy worked, but only when coupled with the special projects designed to help Phelps deal with that adversity.

3% Leaders also understand that projects are in addition to a team's day job. **This is critical**. If something is a consistent or recurring task necessary for everyday business, it is not a project. In general, recurring items within a business are tasks that need to be performed to 1) generate business or 2) support business. Clearly-defined tasks should be described and allocated by job function and job description. We call these tasks "day job" activities. Every organization should strive to formalize day job functions and get them into the most efficient, repeatable process possible.

Looking at projects in this context forces 3% Leaders to narrow the scope of what they are defining in a project. Projects must have the following to be specific to achieving a goal:

    1.   Definition of success

---

13 "Water-Filled Goggles Can't Keep Phelps From Gold Mark" article by Larry Siddons, Aug. 13, 2008, Bloomberg.com.

2. Due date
3. Budget supported by data that considers Time, Money and Resources (TMR)
4. Allocation of internal and external resources

As you identify the right projects needed to propel you toward your vision, you naturally create a habit loop that becomes a powerful force in achieving your goals.

As you identify the right projects needed to propel you toward your vision, you naturally create a habit loop that becomes a powerful force in achieving your goals. Just consider how Phelps' project of swimming blind over and over was a key element in his ultimate success.

Our Leadership System creates projects that are typically 60 to 90 days. We do this so that the practices created in improvement projects will generate good habit loops. Studies of habits conclude that a consistent 60-to-90 day routine will create a habit. 3% Leaders continuously focus on creating good habits and eliminating poor ones.

For more study of habit, I suggest you pick up *The Power of Habit* by Charles Duhigg. It's one of my favorite books. In this book you will learn the power of good and bad habits and how to create good ones. Charles Duhigg put the science behind what 3% Leaders live and practice daily. [14]

---

[14] "The Power of Habit: Why We Do What We Do in Life and Business" by Charles Duhigg, published 2012 by Random House Trade Paperbacks

PRINCIPLE 10. ALIGN YOUR RESOURCES

For a 3% Leader, the right resources are essential. Once you know who you are and where you are going, you're probably going to need some help getting there.

The NFL draft is one of the better examples of aligning resources to achieve a goal. Each spring, general managers and coaches assess their strengths and look to fill gaps with the resources they believe will be needed to achieve their goals.

3% Leaders are constantly performing a role similar to that of NFL general managers and coaches. Internal resources that do not support "day job" functions of a business limit your ability to accomplish projects. In the same way, resources that are not properly aligned with a project, or are not supported appropriately, will derail success every time. Most leaders are frequent offenders in this area. Why is that?

We all do two things pretty consistently. The first is that we naturally tend to think we do more than anyone else in the organization. The second is that we consistently underestimate the time it will take for someone else to do something. The core issue is the same: Others do not have a full appreciation of what we do, and we typically do not have a full appreciation of what we ask of others.

Let's look at aligning resources in the context of Olympic gymnast and gold medalist Gabby Douglas. Gabby Douglas is a wonderful example of an athlete who has achieved her goals. But could Douglas have done this without the help of others? Absolutely not!

As the story goes, Douglas' family went to great lengths supporting her goals and vision. Douglas knew that she would need something different than what she was getting with her local coach in order to achieve her goals. So, Douglas and her mother sought out a resource that would take her talents to the next level. They found a new coach in a different state – a situation that required her to live with another family while she trained. Given the outcome of Douglas' training, it's clear, she and her mother were adept at tapping the right resource.

So it goes in the business world. For a 3% Leader, the right resources deployed in the right way are essential.

> Once you know who you are and where you are going, you're probably going to need some help getting there.

Because once you know who you are and where you are going, you're probably going to need some help getting there.

As a leader, one of your key questions should be, "What resources will you need to achieve what you want?" This simple question begins a deep analysis of how you are actually going to achieve your goals.

3% Leaders intentionally plan and ask their teams to take on new challenges, and **most importantly, do not hesitate to provide the resources needed for success**. They

3% LEADER | 25

acknowledge what they're asking of their team, clearly communicate expectations and solicit input from the team on what they need to be successful.

As I'm sure most of us have seen, when leaders make significant demands of their team without supplying them with the resources they need, they subject themselves to:

- » A false sense of reality
- » Forced dishonesty from their team
- » Turnover
- » Distrust
- » Blame

3% Leaders also understand the value of initially framing any obstacles and reframing them when necessary. They are prepared to offer flexible resources to address the changing environment.

Finally, having a full appreciation of your team's day job is foundational for Principle 10 to be successful.

PRINCIPLE 11. MEASURE WHAT MATTERS

3% Leaders understand the importance of measuring only the few key issues that will make a project a success or a failure.

I have a friend who works for McKinsey Consulting and has developed healthcare analytics technology for the firm. This technology has been wildly successful. Here's the most interesting fact about this technology: It was developed by better interpreting existing rules and regulations. Are you following me? An entirely new business offering was created from interpreting information and establishing a system to measure this data more effectively.

Douglas Hubbard wrote a book on measurement, appropriately titled *"How to Measure Anything."*[15] If you don't care to read the book's 400 pages, here's the point - you don't have an excuse. Many people are reluctant to measure for fear of exact precision. Hubbard would suggest, and I could not agree more, measurement is not about precision but rather reducing uncertainty. Isn't that the point?

Bottom line: Measurement is critical.

Author Simon Sinek suggests, start with the Why.[16]

---

15 "How to Measure Anything: Finding the Value of Intangibles in Business" by Douglas W. Hubbard, published 2014 by John Wiley & Sons, Inc.

16 "Start with Why: How Great Leaders Inspire Everyone to Take Action" by Simon Sinek, published 2009 by the Penguin Group.

Hubbard starts with What. I think they are both correct... what are you measuring and why? These questions may sound simplistic, but often I find people measuring just for the sake of reporting. Clearly, we have access to a tremendous amount of technology used to "measure" progress. That said, if you don't know precisely what you are measuring and why you are measuring, the exercise can be useless.

Let's make it more personal and think about this for a moment: Why would you as a leader create a vision, set a strategy, establish goals, break these goals into digestible projects and allocate valuable resources if you were okay with being uncertain as to the benefit? You wouldn't.

While many minimize the measurement part, that's not acceptable to 3% Leaders.

> 3% Leaders understand that the most important components to measurement are understanding what you are measuring and why.

3% Leaders understand that the most important components to measurement are understanding what you are measuring and why. For example, I once advised a client on a communications strategy designed to "reach the middle" of the organization. When I asked this executive what he meant by "the middle" he did not have an immediate answer. It was time for us to reflect and define who (the what) we would target and why we wanted to target them. Only then could we begin to apply

Hubbard's five-step process for measuring:
1. Define the problem and the relevant uncertainties.
2. Determine what you know now.
3. Compute the value of additional information.
4. Apply the relevant measurement instrument(s) to high-value measurements. (Translation - spend time and effort on what will get you the best information in the most cost-effective manner to help reduce uncertainty in decision-making.).
5. Make a decision and act on it.

So, just get started. Your primary goal with measurement should be to reduce uncertainty in your decisions about your approach and execution. Keep in mind that the real value in measurement does not come from proving accuracy based on your initial observations. Rather, the real value of measurement comes from information gathered to reduce uncertain decisions allowing you to then adapt to circumstances. As a leader, you make decisions knowing you will never have 100 percent of the information desired. This is why measurement is so critical to achieving your goals as a leader. 3% Leaders ensure that understanding *what* they are measuring and *why* they are measuring reduces decision-making uncertainty, which ultimately leads to better decisions.

3% Leaders achieve success through constant analysis and systematic evaluation of a few key points. While they continuously employ precise measurement and reporting based on an initial projected critical path, long-term success comes from monitoring and adjusting as they receive feedback and new information. This may sound academic, but it is the gospel when it comes to measuring success.

So what are you measuring and why? What is your feedback loop to determine if your measurement truly reduces uncertainty in your decisions and approach? When you reduce uncertainty about the activities you have set in place to achieve your vision, strategy and goals, you'll feel more confident in your approach. This confidence builds on itself and you gain momentum. This momentum is what separates 3% Leaders from others.

IMPLEMENTING LEADERSHIP AS A SYSTEM

There's no doubt, leadership is complex. And as I hope I've made clear, the 3% Leader System is not about vision, strategy, goals, projects or measurement in and of themselves. Rather, 3% Leadership is a System that serves to demystify and simplify how top performers achieve their goals and help you refine your own distinct path to management excellence. It is designed with simplicity in mind.

By breaking something that seems complex and overwhelming into three distinct modules, you'll be able to compartmentalize and then sequence what needs to be done. When the 3% Leader System is applied, you'll feel more focused, have more directed work, and achieve success which builds on more success. Gone are the days of walking into your office and wondering what your priorities need to be. The rewards of applying a simple process are limitless.

Remember that 3% Leadership based on *your unique* abilities and leadership design is real. And it's hard to stop real leadership when it's combined with a well-articulated vision, well-designed road map and targeted execution.

ABOUT THE AUTHOR

Carey Rome is a management consultant and speaker on leadership, as well as the founder and CEO of Cypress Resources where he serves as an advisor to executives; a management consultant on strategic projects; and public speaker on the topic of leadership. A certified public accountant (CPA) by trade, Carey understands both value and problem solving. Those attributes are natural and core to him. What was not so natural was leadership. In fact, it took 15 years of intense study and practical lessons for Carey to create the systematic approach to leadership he calls The 3% Leader System. Carey regularly shares his Points of View (POV) on his website and blog.

www.ingramcontent.com/pod-product-compliance
Lightning Source LLC
Chambersburg PA
CBHW030543220526
45463CB00007B/2955